Take-Along Guide

Rocks, Fossils and Arrowheads

by Laura Evert
illustrations by Linda Garrow

NORTHWORD
Minnetonka, Minnesota

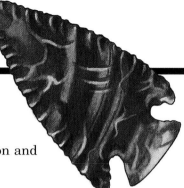

DEDICATION
For Olivia Bruni, whose world of exploration and
discovery is just beginning.

Note to Readers: Under the Archeological Resources Protection Act of
1979, it is illegal to remove arrowheads and other artifacts from public
land without a permit by the Federal land manager.

© NorthWord Press, 2002

NorthWord Books for Young Readers
11571 K-Tel Drive
Minnetonka, MN 55343
www.tnkidsbooks.com

Illustrations by Linda Garrow
Book design by Russell S. Kuepper
Edit by Barbara K. Harold

Library of Congress Cataloging-in-Publication Data

Evert, Laura
    Rocks, fossils, and arrowheads / by Laura Evert; illustrations by LindaGarrow
        p. cm. -- (Take-along guide)
    ISBN 1-55971-786-6 (softcover) 1-55971-805-6 (hardcover)
    1. Rocks--Collection and preservation--Juvenile literature.
    2. Fossils--Collection and preservation--Juvenile literature.
    3. Arrowheads--Collection and preservation--Juvenile
    literature. [1. Rocks--Collection and preservation. 2.
    Fossils--Collection and preservation. 3. Arrowheads--
    Collection and preservation.] I. Garrow, Linda, ill. II. Title.
    III. Series.

    QE433.6.E94 2001
    552'.0075--dc21   2001022215

        Printed in Malaysia

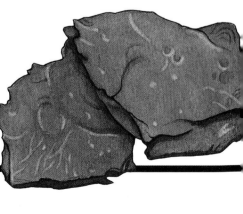

CONTENTS

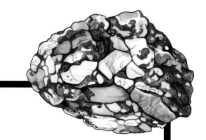

Rocks, Fossils and Arrowheads

INTRODUCTION

Studying rocks, minerals, fossils, arrowheads, and other artifacts can be lots of fun! By learning more about them, you will learn about the history of the earth.

Scientists believe that Earth is over 4.5 billion years old. It is made up of many kinds of minerals, which bind together to form rocks. Depending on which minerals combine and how they are pressed together, they form different kinds of rocks.

Both minerals and rocks come in many different colors and combinations of colors. They may be very hard, or they may be soft or flaky. Some rocks are very smooth, and others are bumpy.

Sometimes, as rocks were forming, plants and animals were trapped inside them. Sometimes their body parts were replaced by other minerals, and then turned to stone. They are called fossils. And they help scientists determine the age of the rock.

Arrowheads and other artifacts were made and used by Native Americans. Heavy rocks were used as tools for grinding and crushing. Softer rocks that were easy to chip into sharp points were used for knives and weapons. Scientists study them to learn about how these people lived.

This Take-Along Guide and its activities will help you find, identify, and learn about the specimens, or samples, you see. You can use the ruler on the back cover to measure what you find. You can bring along a pen or pencil and draw what you see in the Scrapbook.

Have fun exploring the world of Rocks, Fossils and Arrowheads!

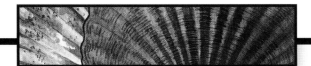

ROCKS & MINERALS

Most rocks are made up of at least two minerals. In addition to making up rocks, individual minerals can form into shapes called crystals. Some crystals are very large and you can easily see them on the surface of the rock. Sometimes the crystals are too small to see without a microscope.

Geologists who study rocks classify them according to how the rocks were formed. The three main types of rock are igneous, sedimentary, and metamorphic.

Hot, liquid magma is found deep in the earth. When it comes to the surface, it is called lava and often flows out of volcanoes. The minerals in magma may cool slowly or quickly. Rocks made in the cooled and hardened magma are called igneous rocks.

Some rocks are formed in water environments. These rocks are often layer upon layer of shells and marine animals that have been compressed together. Or they are pieces of gravel cemented together by sand particles. They are called sedimentary rocks.

Sometimes, deep in the earth, one kind of rock is under such great heat and pressure that it changes into another kind of rock. It may have started out as an igneous or a sedimentary rock. They may look as if they have been squeezed or folded over. These are called metamorphic rocks.

BASALT

WHAT IT LOOKS LIKE

The most common rock on Earth is basalt. It makes up about 70 percent of the Earth's surface. And most of the ocean floor is basalt.

This igneous rock is usually black or very dark gray in color. It is very fine grained, and sometimes you can see dark green crystals.

WHERE TO FIND IT

In wet climates, weathering sometimes turns basalt to clay. In Hawaii, the black sand beaches are made of weathered basalt.

The first lava to come out of a volcano is usually basalt. And it can quickly flow for hundreds of miles, forming thick sheets over the ground.

Basalt is also found where shifting continental plates have pulled and stretched the earth, such as in California, Oregon, Washington, and New Mexico.

Devil's Tower in Wyoming is a very large formation of basalt.

WHAT IT'S USED FOR

Where roads have been cut through areas of basalt, the walls look like big, dark building blocks stacked on top of each other.

Basalt that has been sandwiched between layers of sandstone is called "traprock." This makes a strong rock, and it is often crushed and used for building materials.

Take drinking water with you when you go exploring.

GRANITE

WHAT IT LOOKS LIKE

This igneous rock is usually light in color, with a combination of white, gray, pink, yellow, tan, and possibly flecks of black minerals.

It is coarse-grained, and because the minerals in granite cooled slowly in the magma, larger crystals are visible.

WHERE TO FIND IT

It is usually present where continental plates collided. That is, at the core of old mountains that were formed by the earth folding.

One large outcropping of granite is Yosemite National Park's Half Dome. Because this rock resists weathering, large geological features are usually made of granite. Well-known examples in the United States are Stone Mountain in Georgia and Mount Rushmore in South Dakota.

WHAT IT'S USED FOR

Some gravel is made of granite. Depending on the mineral content, powdered granite can be used as fertilizer.

Slabs of granite can be shined to a smooth finish for tabletops, counters, and floor tiles. Granite may also be used for decorative stone pieces found in buildings.

Monuments, paving blocks, and cemetery markers are often made of granite.

INTERESTING FACTS

A piece of granite that measures about 12 x 12 inches and 3/4 inch thick (30 x 30 x 2 cm) would weigh about 12 to 15 pounds (5 to 7 kg).

8

Use the ruler on the back of this book to measure what you find.

OBSIDIAN

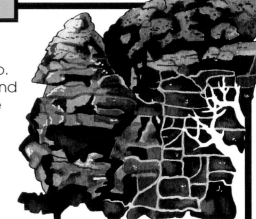

WHAT IT LOOKS LIKE

Obsidian is an igneous rock. It is actually lava that cooled too quickly for individual mineral crystals to be visible. If allowed to cool slowly it would have formed granite.

It has a rich, glassy shine. Most commonly, it is pure black. It can also be lighter brown, brown with some black mottling, and black with a golden or silver sheen.

Obsidian fractures (breaks) easily, so it often has sharp edges. Pieces have a swirl pattern where they were split apart.

into Mexico. It is not found at all in the eastern states.

Over time, obsidian weathers into a dull black color and can have a pitted surface.

WHERE TO FIND IT

It is generally found in small outcrops in western states such as California, Oregon, Utah, and Wyoming, and

INTERESTING FACTS

If some crystals do form inside the obsidan as it cools, it is called snowflake obsidian. Multi-colored obsidian is called rainbow obsidian. Reddish obsidian is sometimes called fire obsidian.

WHAT IT'S USED FOR

Because it is easily fractured it could be made into tools with razor-sharp points, such as knives and heads on spears and arrows.

Today, obsidian is considered to be a semi-precious stone and is used in making jewelry.

Take your time and don't hurry!

RHYOLITE

WHAT IT LOOKS LIKE

This igneous rock is usually pale gray, pink, or yellow. It is fine-grained and contains some larger fragments of minerals and many smaller crystals. Because the rock was cooled very quickly, the smaller crystals are lined up in stripes (called flow-banding).

Sometimes rhyolite rises up through the ground instead of flowing with magma. The rock might form a mound above the ground.

WHERE TO FIND IT

Thousands of square miles are covered by rhyolite in western Texas, Arizona, California, Mexico, Utah, and Oregon. Reddish rhyolite flows can be seen in the area near Las Vegas on the way to the Hoover Dam.

Italy and Ethiopia are also known for having rhyolite deposits.

WHAT IT'S USED FOR

Because of its strength, rhyolite is sometimes cut into blocks and used for constructing buildings. It also can be used to build roads.

One type of rhyolite, called perlite, is used in some types of sound insulation in buildings. It is also the material added to dirt to make commercial potting soil.

As rhyolite cools, the frothy part becomes another rock called pumice. It is very light and has many tiny holes; it looks a little like a sponge. Pumice is the only rock that can float on water.

Tell an adult how long you will be gone.

CONGLOMERATE

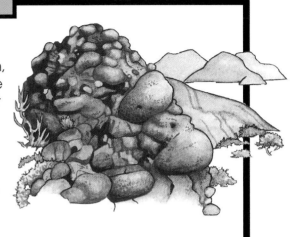

WHAT IT LOOKS LIKE

Conglomerates are sedimentary rocks composed of coarse gravel fragments cemented together by sand that filled in the spaces between the gravel.

The sand was usually supplied by the movement of water in rivers, streams, and waves. But glaciers and even gravity could help to form conglomerates.

The color of conglomerates depends on the color of the gravel and sand. When the fragments are very colorful, conglomerates may be called "puddingstones."

In Van Horn, Texas, there is a deposit many hundreds of feet thick. Specimens can also be found along the Florida Coast and in Massachusetts, California, Montana, and Oregon.

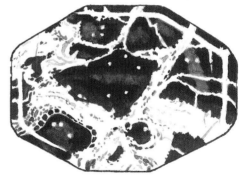

INTERESTING FACTS

Sometimes, gold was found in "looser" conglomerate formations, so old-time miners knew to look in these areas in California and Alaska.

WHERE TO FIND IT

Conglomerates may be found in rivers and on ocean beaches. They are also common in rocky desert areas where water used to be present.

WHAT IT'S USED FOR

Because conglomerates are not very strong, they don't have much commercial use, except for making concrete. But they are sometimes polished as ornamental stone.

LIMESTONE

WHAT IT LOOKS LIKE

Limestone is made from minerals in the shells and bones of marine animals that are no longer alive. Some limestones are made of whole shells cemented together. This dense sedimentary rock is usually light in color. Some varieties can have shades of pink.

It is usually fine-grained, but some can have coarser grains that are visible.

WHERE TO FIND IT

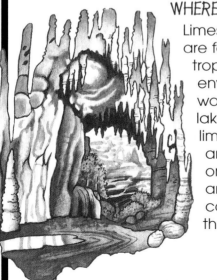

Limestone beds are formed in tropical marine environments and warm freshwater lakes. Sometimes limestone beds are stacked one on top of another, and you can easily see the layering.

Limestone can also be formed in hot water, especially in areas of hot springs and geysers such as in Yellowstone National Park, Wyoming.

The Canadian Rockies, the pyramids of Egypt, and the White Cliffs of Dover, England, are made of types of limestone.

WHAT IT'S USED FOR

In Bermuda, houses are sometimes made of blocks of coquina, which is a type of limestone composed of shell fragments that have turned to stone.

Limestone is an essential part of mortar, the cement that is spread between bricks to hold them together.

Writing chalk is a kind of limestone!

Take this book and a pencil when you go exploring.

SANDSTONE

WHAT IT LOOKS LIKE

Sandstone may be white, gray, or yellow-tan to dark red. Most people are used to seeing light tan to brownish-gray specimens.

It is made up of even-sized grains of sand, which are rounded particles of quartz, closely cemented together. It is a sedimentary rock and you usually can clearly see layers.

WHERE TO FIND IT

You may find sandstone almost everywhere near rivers and lakes, especially in forms such as outcroppings, buttes, and mesas.

It also can be found in desert regions where the earth was once covered with water.

Some sandstone was formed by the wind blowing particles of sand until they were cemented together. They may be seen in the shape of dune walls and other formations, such as the Great White Throne in Zion National Park and Arches National Monument in Utah.

WHAT IT'S USED FOR

Many buildings are made of blocks of sandstone. In the eastern U.S., houses made of sandstone are often called "brownstones."

Sandstone can be crushed and used like sand.

INTERESTING FACTS

Some specimens of sandstone contain fossil fragments, footprints, and even the marks of raindrops.

SHALE

WHAT IT LOOKS LIKE

This sedimentary rock is composed mostly of clay particles. It is also called "mudstone."

Shale can be found anywhere that standing water once existed. Fine particles collect on the bottom of calm water beds and become compressed together. Eventually, other layers form on top.

Distinct layers can be found, sometimes with alternating layers of different colors. Layers can be several feet thick. The layer colors can be gray, to pinkish-purple to dark red, sometimes greenish.

It is a "soft" rock and may break apart when wet. It is easily scratched with a knife and feels smooth and almost greasy to the touch.

WHERE TO FIND IT

The best place to see layered mudstone is in dry, desert areas with little vegetation where roadways have been cut through the earth.

It can be found in almost all delta regions, where moving rivers and streams meet calm bodies of water.

The Painted Desert in Arizona is an example of mudstone layering.

WHAT IT'S USED FOR

Shale is used to make bricks. And it can be used to make ceramics and pottery.

INTERESTING FACTS

Under intense heat some shales yield liquid petroleum. But it's very expensive to process. The earth may hold over 42 trillion gallons (159 trillion liters) of this oil.

To see rocks more easily, carry a plastic magnifying glass with you.

GNEISS

WHAT IT LOOKS LIKE

Gneiss (pronounced "nice") is a metamorphosed, or "changed" rock formed from an igneous rock such as granite. It is made of coarse-grained minerals that are usually visible.

Alternating bands of lighter and darker minerals give it a layered appearance. The layers may look bent or folded. They can be of almost any color, but the more granulated layers are usually lighter in color (white, pink, gray, or tan), while the finer mineral bands are darker (brown or black).

Because gneiss is resistant to weathering, it forms ridges in the landscape that make the terrain look rough and craggy.

WHERE TO FIND IT

Gneiss can be found in the Adirondack regions of New England, south to Georgia. It is also found in the Idaho Batholith area, as well as the Montana and Colorado Rockies.

The region around Great Bear Lake in northwestern Canada is also a good example of a gneiss landscape.

WHAT IT'S USED FOR

There are not many economic uses for gneiss. It can be used for building purposes when composed of weather-resistant minerals.

Polished slabs may be used as interior decorative stone.

MARBLE

WHAT IT LOOKS LIKE

Marble is actually limestone that has been altered by heat and pressure. Because limestone is usually found near marine or ancient marine environments, that's where you will find marble.

Pure marble is white, but since it is a "changed" rock it may have streaks, bands, or vein-like patterns of darker colors.

You will notice it is fine-grained to medium-grained.

WHERE TO FIND IT

Pure marble deposits have been found in Malaga, Spain. One place where marble can be found in the U.S. is Oregon Caves National Monument.

There are also large deposits in Maryland, Vermont, and Georgia.

WHAT IT'S USED FOR

Crushed marble can be used in mixtures of concrete. Statues are often made of marble, and it is used as decoration on the fronts of buildings. When polished, it makes beautiful, decorative stone for columns and tabletops.

The Taj Mahal in India and the Parthenon in Greece are made of marble. So is the Lincoln Memorial in Washington, DC. The Leaning Tower in Pisa, Italy, has many marble panels and columns.

INTERESTING FACTS

In times past, the game of marbles was sometimes played with balls made of polished marble. Today, the marbles are mostly made of glass.

Explore safely. Go with a partner!

SLATE

WHAT IT LOOKS LIKE

Slate is actually shale that has been compressed over time. Pieces of slate are shiny and flat on the top and bottom surfaces, with a darker gray-to-black color.

When slate breaks, it comes apart in sheets. A cross-cut slope of slate looks like layers and layers of blackboards piled up.

WHERE TO FIND IT

Because it is very resistant to weathering, roofs made of slate tiles can be found throughout the world.

Slate is found in mountains, such as the Alps in Europe and the Appalachians in the U.S.

Slate outcroppings can also be found in some areas of California, Pennsylvania, and New York.

WHAT IT'S USED FOR

Schoolroom blackboards used to be made of whole sheets of slate.

Some slate can also be found in shades of green, red, brown, and purple. Tabletops and floor tiles are often made of these colored slates.

Slate is commonly used to make roofing shingles, especially in hot climates. Flagstone paving rocks are actually slate.

Never step into water without first knowing how deep it is.

SCHIST

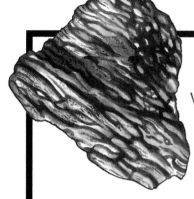

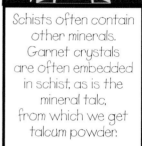

WHAT IT LOOKS LIKE

Schist can be shale, slate, or basalt that has been metamorphosed.

It usually ranges in color from silvery white, many shades of gray, and yellowish to brownish. When weathered, it can have a rusty color.

Up close, schist seems to be made of compressed, flaky pieces of minerals and rock. It has a layered appearance, although not in bands like gneiss. Schist and gneiss are often found together, and sometimes they are layered with each other.

WHERE TO FIND IT

Manhattan Island, New York, is mostly on top of a bed of schist.

Schist can be found with gneiss in the Idaho Batholith area, as well as New England south to Georgia. It is also commonly found in Canada and Scandinavia.

WHAT IT'S USED FOR

Graphite, used now instead of lead in pencils, can be found in schist.

Depending on the mineral content, blocks of schist may be used as building stones. Sometimes it is crushed and used as gravel.

One type of schist is cut into slabs and used as roofing for houses in the Alps of Europe.

Get permission before going onto someone's land.

GARNET

WHAT IT LOOKS LIKE

There are different kinds of this mineral. The ones most people recognize are crimson red to brown in color. Some of them are yellow, green, black, or even clear. Sometimes they may seem to change color in different light.

It was named after the Latin word *granalus* for "pomegranate" because this fruit's seeds are a deep red color.

WHERE TO FIND IT

Garnets are commonly found in igneous and metamorphic rocks such as marble and schist throughout the world.

Gem-quality garnets have been found in Arizona, Utah, Idaho, Alaska, Maine, and North Carolina. Garnets also can be found in many other countries and regions of the world such as Russia, the Czech Republic, Australia, Scandinavia, and South America.

In South Africa, the garnet is called the Cape Ruby.

WHAT IT'S USED FOR

Garnets have been used as a decorative stone since around 5000 B.C. in Egypt. During the Middle Ages they became even more valued as a gemstone.

Some garnets are ground up and used as the abrasive surface on sandpaper.

Garnet is the birthstone for the month of January.

Stay safe! Don't go near the edges of cliffs and outcroppings.

19

MICA

WHAT IT LOOKS LIKE

Mica is one of the most abundant of rock-forming minerals. It may be found in any of the three types of rock.

It breaks into sheets that can be thinner than a fingernail and translucent. The sheets are somewhat flexible and don't break easily.

There are two forms of mica. Muscovite may be colorless or white to pale yellow to gray. Biotite is usually dark brown to dark green to black because it contains lots of iron. Biotite is less common than Muscovite.

WHERE TO FIND IT

Micas can be found almost everywhere. Utah, California, the Black Hills of South Dakota, and the New England states have large deposits. They are also found in Brazil, India, Scandinavia, and Switzerland.

WHAT IT'S USED FOR

Muscovite was once called Muscovy glass and was used to make the windows of stoves, lanterns, and fuse plugs. It was also used to make electrical insulation in appliances like household irons and toasters.

Some types of house paint contain mica. These paints are usually labeled "fireproof."

Always wear shoes or boots to protect your feet.

QUARTZ

WHAT IT LOOKS LIKE

This is the most common mineral on Earth. It has a glassy appearance and can be found in almost every color. Rock crystal quartz is colorless and looks like ice. Many specimens are banded.

Quartz forms six-sided crystals (hexagons) and usually has pyramid-shaped ends. Some crystals can be huge, weighing many tons.

WHERE TO FIND IT

Quartz is an important rock-forming mineral. It can be found in granite, sandstone, and gneiss.

It can be found throughout the world. Especially large quartz crystals have been found in Brazil.

Much of the dust in the air consists of quartz.

WHAT IT'S USED FOR

Clear rock crystal quartz generates an electrical charge. It is a very important element of radios, telephones, and wrist watches.

Quartz is the main component of sand. Sand is a major component of glass.

Flint is black quartz. It was used to make sparks that could start fires.

Many different colors of quartz are used as jewelry. Citrine is yellow quartz. Amethyst is a purple gemstone that is a kind of quartz. It is the birthstone for February.

INTERESTING FACTS

On the Frederich Mohs scale of hardness, a diamond is a #10 and quartz is a #7. Your fingernail is only a #2.

Make Some Rock Candy

If you like sugar, you will really like these crystal "rock" formations.
They are not only fun to make, they taste delicious!

WHAT YOU NEED

▼

- A clean glass jar
- A piece of clean cotton string
- A large paper clip
- A popsicle stick
- Scissors
- 1 cup of water
- A medium saucepan
- A wooden spoon
- 3 or 4 cups of white granulated sugar
- An adult to help you

WHAT TO DO

▼

1 Wash and dry the paper clip. Tie it to one end of the string.

2 Tie the other end of the string to the middle of the popsicle stick.

3 Moisten the string with cool water.

4 Rest the popsicle stick across the opening of the jar, letting the string with the paperclip hang down into the jar. Make sure the paperclip does not touch the bottom of the jar.

5 With an adult's help, heat 1 cup of water in the saucepan until it boils. Remove the pan from the heat.

6 When the water stops bubbling, slowly pour the sugar into the water.

7 Stir the water and sugar mixture with the spoon until all or most of the sugar is dissolved.

8 Let the mixture cool for a few minutes, then have an adult pour it into the jar with the string.

9 Set the jar in a place where it won't be disturbed, and you can watch the crystals grow.

The sugar will begin to turn into rock candy in just a few hours. The rock crystals will continue growing for several days. You can eat the candy off the string anytime you wish, but the longer you wait, the bigger the candy will be!

OTHER IDEAS:

• You can add a few drops of flavoring, such as mint or vanilla extract, to the sugar-water mixture before you pour it into the jar.

• You also can add food coloring. Stir one or two drops into the sugar-water before it goes into the jar.

FOSSILS

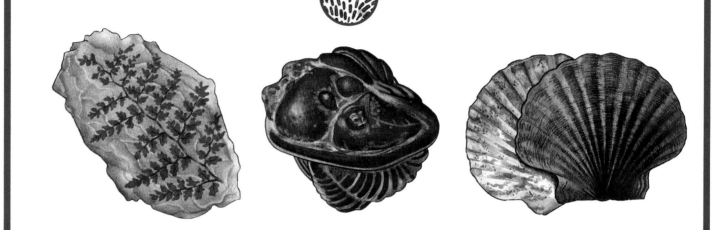

When most plants and animals die, they just rot away, back into the earth, until nothing is left. But sometimes they are completely trapped or covered in mud or sand that turns to rock. Eventually, the rock holding the fossil cracks open or weathers away and the fossil can be found.

Most fossils were sea creatures with shells that are found today in sedimentary rock, such as sandstone and limestone. That means they can be found in areas that used to be water environments. You may find a single fossilized shell or a cluster of shells cemented together.

A whole tree may become a fossil. Its pieces are called petrified wood, and they may be different colors.

Some fossils are not the whole animal or plant, but just its imprint or outline. This kind of fossil may look like a foot print, or tail print, or leaf print.

The oldest fossil ever found is over 3 billion years old! Fossils are still being made every day. Years from now someone will find a shell or plant fossil from today and be able to learn about the things that lived during our lives.

PLANT FOSSILS

WHAT THEY LOOK LIKE

As rocks formed over thousands of years, plants were trapped inside of them. These plant fossils are valuable to scientists because knowing when the plant lived can help determine the age of the rock.

One way plants may become fossils is by carbonization. This is when the natural oils within the plant seep out, leaving a thin layer of carbon on the rock as it was forming. Commonly found plant fossils are the leaf imprints of eucalyptus, ginkgo, ferns, and palms.

Petrification is another way plants are fossilized. This happens when minerals inside the plant's cells crystallize and become hard. This is how petrified wood is created.

Up close, petrified trees look and feel like solid stone. Because the minerals in petrified wood can contain many colors, it sometimes looks painted or iridescent.

INTERESTING FACTS

Paleontologists are scientists who study fossils. They have even found whole, fossilized pine cones.

WHERE TO FIND THEM

Plant fossils can be found almost everywhere in many different kinds of rock. Coal beds in particular may contain them. Plant fossils usually are not found in wet, swampy areas, however, because the plants probably deteriorated too quickly to be preserved.

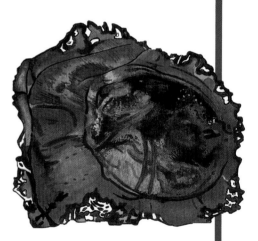

BIVALVES

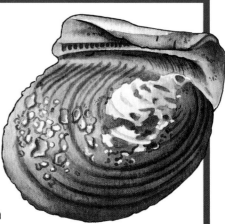

WHAT THEY LOOK LIKE

Clams, mussels, scallops, and oysters are called bivalves because they have left-side and right-side shells. A bivalve's two shells are usually the same size and are nearly identical to each other.

While they are alive, bivalves sometimes burrow into sand or the soft sediment of the water bed. Over time, the sediment may compress into rock, trapping the bivalve inside and forming a fossil.

After the animal inside the shell dies, the muscle holding the two shells together relaxes, and the shells may come apart. So sometimes only half of the bivalve is found.

WHERE TO FIND THEM

All bivalves are aquatic, meaning that they live in or near the water. They may be found in both freshwater and saltwater. They are mostly found in shallow areas. Oysters are the most common bivalve found.

Bivalve shells may be tiny—smaller than 1 inch (2.5 cm) across—and some may be large—more than 1 foot (30 cm) across!

Since they live in many different aquatic environments, fossilized bivalves can be found in different kinds of rock, such as sandstone, shale, and limestone.

INTERESTING FACTS

Bivalves have been used as food since prehistoric times. Their fossil records go back over 600 million years.

A hat with a brim will protect you from sunburn.

BRACHIOPODS

WHAT THEY LOOK LIKE

Lampshells and spiriferids are examples of brachiopods, which have top and bottom shells.

If you drew an imaginary line down the center of a brachiopod, the two sides would look nearly identical, except that one would be larger. Most brachiopods are less than 5 inches (13 cm) across, but some are almost 1 foot (30 cm) across.

Brachiopods have strong muscles that hold the two shells together, even after the animal inside dies. So you are likely to find a brachiopod fossil with both shells.

WHERE TO FIND THEM

Brachiopods move around less than bivalves, and some cannot move by themselves at all. They rely on the water's currents to transport them. Some brachiopods attach themselves to the floor of the ocean and remain in that one place their whole lives. A few brachiopods burrow into the muddy bottom.

Brachiopods sometimes join together. Whole groups of fossilized brachiopods have been found cemented in rock. Limestone, shale, and sandstone are just some of the rocks in which they have been found.

INTERESTING FACTS

When brachiopods find a surface to live on, they grab on with a "foot," called a pedicle.

BRYOZOANS

WHAT THEY LOOK LIKE

Living bryozoans can be found on most seashores, as well as in deep water. They are called aquatic "moss animals." Each individual bryozoan is only about 1 mm long. It would take twenty-five of them to measure 1 inch (2.5 cm).

Some bryozoans attach to each other and form groups called colonies that look like fan-shaped, lacy leaves. Other colonies look like little branched twigs. A whole bryozoan colony may be only 1 or 2 inches (2.5 to 5 cm) across. Larger colonies can be 2 feet (61 cm) across.

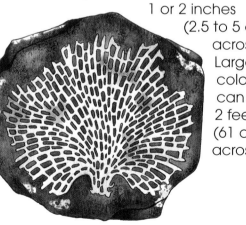

WHERE TO FIND THEM

Fossilized bryozoans are often found in specimens of shale. Thousands of years ago, many colonies of bryozoans inhabited the oceans. They looked like a mossy field swaying in the water currents. As layer upon layer of sediment formed on the ocean floor, they hardened and compressed into shale, or became limestone. The colonies of bryozoans were trapped between the layers and became fossilized.

Bryozoans usually attach themselves to hard objects, such as rocks, in shallow waters. They also may attach themselves to ships, pilings, piers, and docks.

INTERESTING FACTS

The common name of a bryozoan may come from its appearance, such as porcupine, bushy, hairy, and black-speckled.

Use patience and sharp eyesight to find fossils.

TRILOBITES

WHAT THEY LOOK LIKE

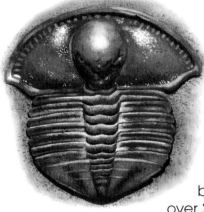

Trilobites were very common marine animals before they became extinct over 200 million years ago. Scientists believe there were thousands of species, or kinds, of trilobites. Some were very tiny and some grew as long as 3 feet (0.9 m).

They had many legs and hard outer shells, called exoskeletons, that were either smooth or edged with spines.

Trilobites had to shed their outer shells in order to grow. So some trilobite fossils are not the entire animal, but only their old shell.

WHERE TO FIND THEM

Trilobites lived in shallow waters throughout the world. They were mostly bottom-dwellers, where they could burrow into the sand and mud to hide or find food. Some fossils show the trail and tracks a trilobite left as it moved along.

When trilobites defended themselves, they would roll up into a ball. Some have been found in rock this way. Also, trilobites were very social, and groups of them have been found fossilized together. Limestone and shale are the best rocks for finding trilobite fossils. Billions of them have been found in the Wheeler Shale Formation in Utah.

INTERESTING FACTS

Trilobites lived and became extinct even before dinosaurs roamed the earth. They are ancient relatives of today's horseshoe crabs, spiders, and cockroaches.

Stay away from poison ivy and poison oak when you explore.

Create Your Own Fossil

You can make a "secret" fossil by yourself. Or you can make fossils
with your family or friends. Even your pet can have a fossil of its own!

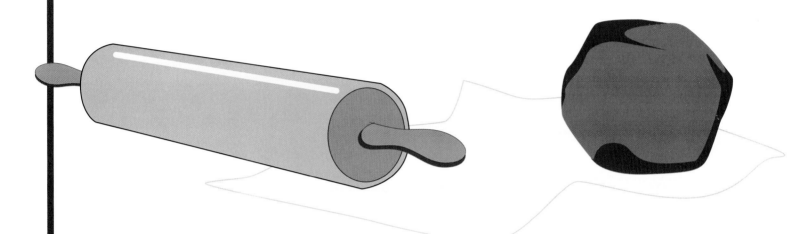

WHAT YOU NEED

▼

- Modeling clay
- Newspapers
- Waxed paper
- An old rolling pin
- A pencil or toothpick

WHAT TO DO

▼

1 Cover the top of a table with newspapers.

2 Put a large piece of waxed paper right in front
of you on the table.

3 Squeeze the clay in your hands until it becomes
soft. Then set it on the waxed paper.

4 With your hands, roll the clay into a smooth ball.

5 Press the ball flat, removing any air bubbles.

6 Make the clay into any shape you like, such as a square, rectangle, triangle, or circle.

7 Use the rolling pin to make the clay flat and even. Use your hands to help keep the shape. Do not make it too thin or too big. You should be able to pick it up without bending or tearing it.

8 Gently press your hand into the clay deep enough to leave a good print. Slowly lift up your hand. If you pressed hard enough you should be able to see lines and fingerprints in the clay.

9 Next, use the pencil or toothpick to "write" your name and the date you made the fossil.

10 Set the fossil in a place where it can completely dry out. It may take several days.

OTHER IDEAS:

• You can also press leaves into the clay to make plant fossils. Use leaves that are thick and sturdy and that don't tear easily. Choose leaves that have thick veins or interesting edges.

Now you're ready to turn your clay into a true fossil! Find a place outside where you have permission to dig. Pick a spot that usually stays dry and is not near water. Dig a deep hole and carefully place your fossil inside. Cover it with dirt, gently packing the dirt so there are no air spaces. If no one disturbs your fossil, someone may find it hundreds of years from now.

• If you want to keep your fossil, you can paint it and use it as a paperweight or give it as a gift to someone special.

ARROWHEADS & ARTIFACTS

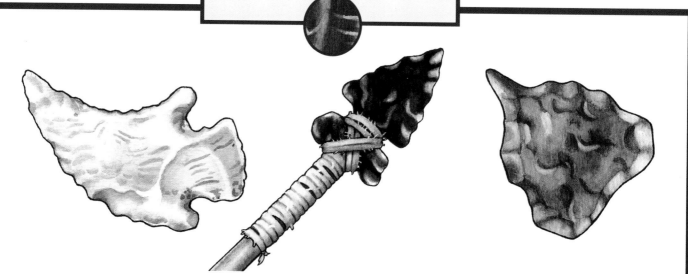

When early people needed tools and weapons, they made many of them from stones and sticks that they found close to where they lived. For almost as long as humans have been on the Earth, they have made tools and weapons in order to build shelter, hunt for food, and defend themselves.

In North America, there are clues to how the early Native Americans lived. These clues are found every time a person discovers a kind of Indian artifact.

Different tribes in different areas used different materials and different shapes for their tools and weapons. Many items were formed from igneous rock because it is very strong. Some were made from softer sedimentary rock because it could be sharpened into a point.

Heavy rocks were often used for axes or hammers. Lighter and smaller rocks were used for more delicate work, such as poking holes in pieces of an animal hide to sew them together for clothing.

KNIVES

Knives were used for many of the same purposes as they are used today. They were needed to cut food, leather, and the materials that were used when sewing leather together. Many small knives had more than one sharp edge, so they were flaked or chiseled on both sides. In contrast, our knives of today have only one sharp edge.

INTERESTING FACTS

Native Americans used a variety of tools to carve pictures on stone called petroglyphs. These rock art drawings were often very large and made on cave walls.

Some knives were notched so they could be attached to wooden handles. Early knives were oblong shaped or pear shaped with one end wider to grasp it with the hand. Many of them were about 4 to 5 inches (10 to 13 cm) long. Some were as long as 9 inches (22 cm). Large knives usually only had one very sharp edge.

Even when found today, many ancient knives are still sharp enough to be used. Sometimes knives are found with coarse edges, or with serrations that look like tiny teeth. These knives were used as saws.

Remember to leave arrowheads and artifacts where you find them.

33

ARROWHEADS

Most arrowheads found today are between 1/2 inch (1.25 cm) and 2 inches (5 cm) long. It is likely that small ones were attached to small sticks for hunting birds. Large ones on stronger pieces of wood were probably used to hunt larger animals.

Most regions had just one type of flint, and most arrowheads found in that area were made in one shape. Because flint can be white, gray, red, or black, arrowheads can be different colors.

Arrowheads were usually made out of a hard sedimentary rock called flint. There are different types of flint in North America so you may find different types of arrowheads in different parts of the continent.

An arrowhead has three parts. The sharp end is called the tip, or point. The wide middle section is called the body, or face. The square end is called the base or bottom. Often when a person finds an arrowhead in a field or near a stream, the arrowhead is broken. It might be missing the tip or base, or both.

When exploring at night, take a flashlight.

When pieces of flint chip off, the edges are sharp. Those edges of the arrowhead are beveled, or sloped, by carefully striking it with another very hard rock. This makes the edge thin and even sharper.

Many arrowheads have a notch on each side where the body and base meet. Arrowheads are notched in different ways. For example, some arrowheads are side-notched while others are bottom-notched or corner-notched. And others may be notched in more than one place.

Don't put your hand into any hole or burrow. It may be an animal's home.

SPEAR POINTS

An artifact that is larger than 2 inches (5 cm) and looks like an arrowhead is called a spear point. It may be even longer than 3 inches (7.5 cm). Spears were used in hunting animals for food. They were made of long pieces of wood with a sharp "point" attached to one end. Spears could be thrown or carried by hand.

Most spear points do not have notches for attaching to the spear shaft. The edges away from the sharp end were usually ground smooth so they could be attached to wooden spears without cutting through the binding material. In addition to flint, some spear points were made of obsidian, quartz, or buffalo bone.

INTERESTING FACTS

Spear points were invented several hundred years before arrow-heads. They date back as far as 7500 B.C.

If spear points or arrowheads became chipped or broken during use, they were often remade into other small tools such as knives or scrapers.

Tell an adult where you are going, or take one with you.

AXES

One of the largest artifacts you may find is a stone axe. These were often made out of granite, slate, or iron ore, but not flint. Other harder stones were used to grind the axe stone, forming a wedge shape with one sharp side.

The large groove near the blunt end of the axe was used to help fasten it to a handle. The groove could be shallow or deep, wide or narrow, straight or angled.

The weight of an axe may range from 1 pound (0.45 kg) to 20 pounds (9 kg). The size could be small for easy jobs, or large for difficult jobs. Their main purpose was to cut and chop wood for fires and building materials. They were also important in constructing shelters. The blunt or back end of a heavy axe was sometimes used as a hammer.

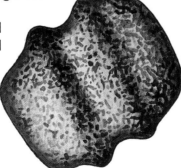

Small axes without grooves were used without a handle and are called "celts." These hand axes were very smooth for a more comfortable grip. They were used for chopping smaller objects like branches and twigs.

INTERESTING FACTS

Axes are commonly found in the Midwest where there were vast forests. They were sometimes used to form a dug-out, or canoe, from the trunk of a fallen tree.

Wear a hat and use sunscreen to protect yourself from the sun.

DRILLS AND AWLS

In their everyday lives, early people needed to make holes in animal hides, softer stones, and wood. In order to do this they made tools that they could use to puncture through these materials.

A drill was usually notched to attach it to the end of a stick. To make a hole, the pointed end was placed on the material and the stick was rotated back and forth by rubbing it between the hands.

Drills were often made of broken arrowheads or bones of animals. Because a drill is much narrower than the body of an arrowhead, it was perfect for recycling into this new use. Sometimes they were made of petrified wood. They could be as long as 4 inches (10 cm).

Awls can be as long as drills but they are not as narrow. They are more triangular in shape and have no notches. Awls were almost always made of flint and they were made to be held in the hand. A depression was often carved in one side for the thumb of the person who was using it. This made it easier to grip.

Use insect repellent to protect yourself.

SCRAPERS

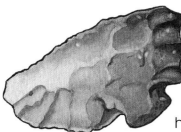

Scrapers were used in preparing many kinds of food, as well as hides for clothing and shelter. They were also used to make other tools out of animal bones.

Pieces of quartz and flint were used as scrapers. They have one edge that is much thinner than the other edges. To make a scraper sharper, it would be flaked only on one side, leaving the other side smooth.

They may be as small as a thumbnail or large enough to be gripped in the whole hand. Scrapers were often oval or round. Different shapes worked better for different uses.

An indentation for a thumb is often seen where the person using the scraper would need to grip it. The handle side is smooth.

Scrapers were not usually resharpened. When one scraper became dull from the work, Indians simply made another to continue the job.

Design a Friendship Necklace

WHAT TO DO

▼

1 Mold your clay into the shape of an arrowhead using the pictures in this book as your guide. Then allow your clay arrowhead to completely dry.

2 Lay the three long pieces of yarn together, stretched out straight. Tie them together in a knot at one end.

3 Braid the three pieces of yarn, starting at the knot end. Make sure the braid is not too loose. When you finish the braid, tie the loose ends together in another knot.

4 Wrap the middle of the short piece of yarn around the arrowhead at the notches. Criss-cross and tie the yarn to make sure the arrowhead is tied tight.

5 Tightly tie the ends of the short yarn to the center of the braided yarn, so the arrowhead hangs down a little.

6 Tie the ends of the braid together to make a necklace that you can slip over your head.

You can give your necklace as a gift to a special friend. Or you could make two matching necklaces for you and your pal as a sign of friendship!

OTHER IDEAS:

• Instead of yarn, you can use ribbon, string, cloth strips, or long shoelaces for your necklace.

• You can also use shorter pieces and make a bracelet, key chain, or bookmark.

WHAT YOU NEED

▼

• 3 pieces of yarn, each about 36 inches (1 m) long

• 1 piece of yarn about 15 inches (38 cm) long

• Modeling clay and supplies from fossil activity on pages 30-31

• Scissors

Make a Rock Display

WHAT YOU NEED

▼

- Your rock collection
- Soap, water, and an old toothbrush
- A soft towel
- An empty egg carton
- Cotton balls
- Small pieces of paper for note tags
- A pen or pencil
- Liquid glue

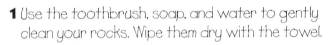

WHAT TO DO

▼

1 Use the toothbrush, soap, and water to gently clean your rocks. Wipe them dry with the towel.

2 Place a cotton ball in each of the egg carton holes. Lay one rock on top of each cotton ball.

3 Make a note on a piece of paper for each rock. It could say what type of rock it is and where and when you found it.

4 Put a dot of glue on the back of the paper. Press it on the cotton beside its rock.

Now your collection won't get lost or damaged. And it's ready to show to your family and friends!

OTHER IDEAS:

• If your rocks are too big to fit in the holes of an egg carton, you can use a shoe box with a lid. The cotton balls can cover the entire bottom of the box, and the rocks can be placed on them as they will fit.

• You can make another display box for other treasures you find.

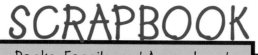

SCRAPBOOK
Rocks, Fossils and Arrowheads

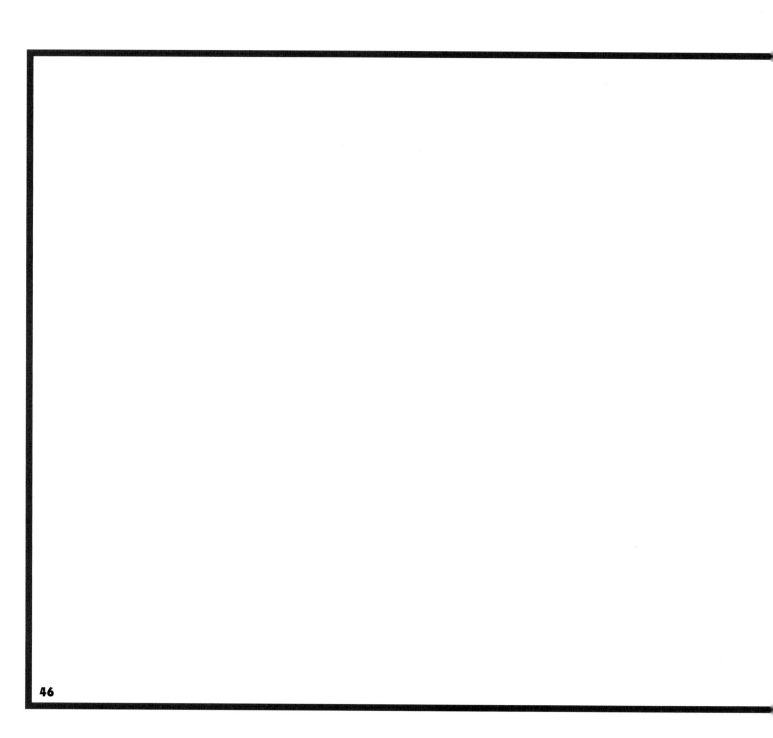

Find All Kinds of Stuff . . .

Take-Along Guides

Titles available in the Take-Along Guide series:

Berries, Nuts and Seeds
ISBN 978-1-55971-573-7

Birds, Nests and Eggs
ISBN 978-1-55971-624-6

Caterpillars, Bugs
and Butterflies
ISBN 978-1-55971-674-1

Flamingos, Loons
and Pelicans
ISBN 978-1-55971-943-8

Frogs, Toads and Turtles
ISBN 978-1-55971-593-5

Planets, Moons and Stars
ISBN 978-1-55971-842-4

Rabbits, Squirrels
and Chipmunks
ISBN 978-1-55971-579-9

Rocks, Fossils
and Arrowheads
ISBN 978-1-55971-786-1

Seashells, Crabs
and Sea Stars
ISBN 978-1-55971-675-8

Snakes, Salamanders
and Lizards
ISBN 978-1-55971-627-7

Tracks, Scats and Sign
ISBN 978-1-55971-599-7

Trees, Leaves and Bark
ISBN 978-1-55971-628-4

Wildflowers, Blooms
and Blossoms
ISBN 978-1-55971-642-0

NorthWord
Minnetonka, Minnesota